ODDEST & OLDEST & SADDEST & BEST

ODDEST & OLDEST & SADDEST & BEST

Jane Zwart

ORISON
BOOKS

Oddest & Oldest & Saddest & Best

ISBN: 978-1-949039-68-9

Orison Books
PO Box 8385
Asheville, NC 28814
www.orisonbooks.com

Cover art: "L'Humeur Vagabonde (Restless Mood)" by Joseph Cornell copyright © 2025 The Joseph and Robert Cornell Memorial Foundation. Licensed by VAGA at Artists Rights Society (ARS), New York. Photo provided by The National Gallery of Art.

Cover design by Luke Hankins and Addison Skigen.

Manufactured in the U.S.A.

ORISON
BOOKS

CONTENTS

III

*for the people who laid the foundations
of all that I love: Dad, Mum, Adam, Luke*

Poem with a Hole in It

My great-aunt had a typewriter that punched the paper belly
from every O she wrote. Every poem has a hole in it.

A rifle's sight, the peg of lens in a motel door. The circle
cut in a kaleidoscope so we can see colors petaling

down the tube. Your pupil guzzling
data and light, my pupil guzzling data and light.

I think of the divots left in a birthday cake when the kid
uproots the candles. I think of the pocks Christmas lights burn

into a porch rail's ruff of snow. We are on different sides
of this eyelet. My great-aunt taught me that. Every poem

is riddled with holes. But I am threading two tin cans'
punctured ends that you might know me yet.

I

All my life I was a bride married to amazement

after Mary Oliver's "When Death Comes"

When death comes, final and novel—
the trick cul-de-sac or burst dam, a door
that opening erases or shutting disappears—
I want to watch the filmstrip once more.

I want to see the caterpillar, his whole body
a fat neck, rolling hills and horripilation.
I want to remember how, every time
he dropped from some leaf to my arm,
we appalled each other. I want to remember
how, every time, astonishment
made us the same.

When death comes, I want to watch,
reel-to-reel, my unrealized fears
yielding to what I never thought to dread:
meningitis, oily rags.

I want to flip back to the times
my name came up lucky
in the raffle of who-gets-to-see-herons.

All my life I was a bride married to amazement:
every sickness an affront, every peach
a geode. All my life: bowled over by every hell—
fresh, stale, it didn't matter—

and all my life blown about, a feather
on the breath of God.
When it's over, I want to say: it was a requited love.

But probably, even then, I won't know
whether I have passed my life as surprise's adept
or her dupe.

Probably, even then, I'll only
be sure of falling asleep
beside my strange bedfellow, strange.

Life Imitates

Storm King Art Center, New Windsor, NY

We knew some of it was sculpture,
the marbles and mobiles. The bronze
diptych, two doors standing upright

and open, hinged to one another, yoked,
a book, each of its opposing pages
the other's negative, each a collage

of wedge and gouge so perfect
we never did decide which was
the mold and which was the cast. Yes,

and the wall was a sculpture, halving
a hill, unless it was us, ascending
on opposite sides; dry-stacked, it cut

through a pond; a heavy ribbon
when it slalomed a picket of oaks.
The benches were sculpture too:

on one, a groundskeeper left his gloves
or a weak-wristed god his hands,
they were larger than life, were they

sandstone? For hours, we were sure
all of it was art. A gully full of stake flags—
yellow for steam, purple for slurry,

surveyors' pinks, plumbers' blues—
it was an installation, new and near
the museum's earliest gift, a mudrock

upholstered in moss. I'm telling you,
it was catching. I stared at the likeness
of a whistlepig and when she bounded

into the milkweed, I stood, astonished,
in her stead, next in a relay of statues.
But even now, cormorants are topping

utility poles with acanthus, and on full
trains tall kids are draping the laps
of mothers with tragical faces.

Long Distance

Once my mom and I fought
about the distance to Ann Arbor.
It isn't the city where my brother
died. It's the city where a hospital
failed to scrape or poison or radiate
his small body back to health.
And that was enough. My mom
stopped thinking of that city
as an acceptable place. I didn't.
We fought.
                    Neither of us
would believe only small things
hung in the balance. I was desperate
to hear plaintive music and, more,
to outsmart my mother like I would
a garage door, pushing a button
and dancing out of range, over
her shelter's failsafes. My mom
was desperate to keep me from dying.

We fought in my childhood bedroom.
I remember her face, her fury.

. . .

This afternoon I scolded my son away
from Mount Major's steep places. I knew
I was embarrassing. I did not care.

I have come to the edge of myself
and here can see how some furies
are also love. And how love, where

everything hangs in the balance,
can think of this as an acceptable trade:
despise me, but survive.

Morbid Children

Some are born morbid.
Some, as soon as they know a flower
for a flower, know what browning
means. The most precocious

see the baby's breath waste
in the vase and make the leap—
that will also happen to me—

whereas most can grieve
the death of a dog
without grasping
the rampant synecdoche.

For my brother it was E.T.'s ribs,
his nightlight heart. For me
it was my brother's baldness
adding wattage to his eyes.

My childhood was not an agony

but I agonized anyway, my wakefulness the rail
that kept my parents' dark blue car uncrushed
by matching nights, my vigilance a warranty

for music boxes' transmissions:
                                        I destined
their tiny engines and tinny songs to end
both at once, timed their tuned combs' coasting
to a stop in pin drums' seams. My childhood

was not an agony—not at all—but fitting a pair
of wheels to the car wash's tracks, yielding
to the crush of gallop brushes, dervish pine trees,
I still fear for my parents driving in darkness

and I still watch as mitter curtains sweep
wet braille from my windshield, gently
obliterating untended songs and think how strange
the pang of metal waltzes failing to resolve.

Pink Noise Machine

The ear knows the river—
even the river made methodical,
flumed and dammed—

from an untuned radio.
It knows white noise, an oxbow
bolo of electric burs,

from pink. Pink static
runs on moonbeams. Consider
the ocean, its sough,

its surf. A lunar crank
spins water into waves and slides
tides in and out.

The ear knows families
of sounds. It knows the motor
that pocks mute night

from the tranquil growl
of swells and rills and westerlies.
Only pink can a current

sound like envelopes
rattling their cellophane windows
the nights your dad paid bills.

Learning to Read

Against what does one break
the ampoule of a word?

Almost never can you crack
the glass, the phonic code

by shutting the book
around the capsule, hard,

as one would shell a nut
between a wood doll's jaws.

Books are full of tulle
and sawdust and most words

resist brute force
and roll, whole and still

secret from their chapters
into your lap. Sometimes

you can hull a word
syllabically, bulb by bulb,

and the sound inside each aril
will hold its shape

long enough for you
to pop it in your mouth

and, as with the beads
freed from a pomegranate,

you can break the juice
from the seeds with your teeth.

Yes, to swallow some phial
along with the philter

is almost a sure thing
but the small harm that does

is good practice. Keep boring
your way into the glass flasks

and soon, soon you will find
the vial's foil and pull its seal,

cleanly, and drink. Soon
you'll trade the little vessel in,

soon swig from the bottle
crammed with a ship, soon drain

the snow globe, soon press your lips
to the dipper annealed in stars.

Used Benison

Tonight I am borrowing a septuagenarian's life,
his lap full of husks and silk, his friend running
street lights; they are rushing ears of sweetcorn

to boiling water, they are racing sugar's corrosion
into starch. I am borrowing everything. The chrysalis
a boy set on his dresser for its shape alone. The brief

pet it bred. I am trying on a whole record of wonder:
the child's, an inning into summer; the groom's,
his paisley a distraction to the Baptists; the old fellow's—

if this is life who could earn their keep?—when he throws
up his hands. There is a joy that helpless. I borrow it.
I too have been loved more than makes sense.

Waiting Room

It is possible to pass a whole life
like this, half-harkening,
perusing a backlog of *Vanity Fair*.

It is possible to hang on the turn
of a knob without wanting
the thing on the door's other side.

You could grow old here, your sight
skating the eights that ivy up
the wallpaper while reruns run.

It is possible to pass years waiting,
unyearning, and still to start
at a voice announcing your name.

Midlife Crisis

Some rivers you put into trusting to the livery
downstream, to the hirelings who will wade
into the shallows and hand you from kayak
to bank; I thought that was the deal I'd made

with time: that I would live until interrupted,
that I would be swept where the current said
and at the last alight. How strange, then,
to learn that being was a palindrome I'd read

to its hairpin middle. I thought it was a river—
how strange, hull spun on a backwater, to learn
that my route ran out and back, to feel myself
grow younger. I did not think I would yearn

for the silver to change to rust, to be as beautiful
bent double, unsteady again. Well, now I know
the tributaries of Adam's ale. Now, unable to forget
there will be an end, with awful strength, I row.

Bad news finds you where it finds you,

Sarah says. She is not wrong. Every day
diagnoses steal through routine's transoms.
Every day people weep unwillingly

in elevated trains, in classrooms,
in a surfeit of natural light. My grandma
died, and my phone rang in an arcade.

I made my mom repeat herself. I made
my son loose, on his birthday, my hand.
Once, bad news had to strive more.

It used a solemn buddy system and landlines;
it had to find us home. Not anymore.
It finds us wherever it finds us,

Sarah says. She is not appalled. She knows:
it wouldn't do a lick of good for us,
subpoenaed by grief, to juke its messenger.

She knows chances are we'll run, unsuspecting,
toward the ones who tell us it's now:
the end of the world. And how could it be

otherwise? Bad news, our dear ones will say,
in the same voices that have said See you
and Remember. Bad news, giving the words

to the only air there is, ambered by kisses
and smudged by fire and reserved,
in equal measure, for first and last breaths.

I read that the moon is rusting

My son defines time—its river, not its measure—
as the way one event changes into another.

I am letting what my son knows of time
climb and turn a laddered wheel in my mind.

I am letting the river run the mill that changes
one kind of unknowing into another.

. . .

Once a student told me that her mother kept
vases of flowers long past their prime.

She thought them still beautiful, wizened tulips,
their petals knuckling into pecans.

. . .

I read that the moon is rusting. Here on earth
a breeze kicked up by passing cars

fans a dead katydid. Invisible thumbs shuffle
her wings' gauzy underthings.

. . .

One event is turning into another. My son grows
tall but is still young enough to trail

a hand, offhandedly, in the current that carries him.
There is so little we can demand from time

but I would ask to be like a tulip, like a katydid,
like the henna-chinned moon:

one of those who, done or undone, changes
into another kind of wonder.

II

On Beauty and Being Just

It is possible I have been unfair
to them, the flamboyants:
to opals, to abalones, to moths
more phosphorescent
than any eyeshadow I've worn—
because who knows?

Maybe the painted bunting
would willingly trade
his layered, paint-by-number capes
for the robin's rusty apron. Maybe
the hibiscus isn't a satellite dish
tilting on its stem to overhear
the praise of passers-by
but an umbrella mortified
that day has left it open
in a narrow place to dry. Maybe
the Northern Lights' magic
is static, escaped photons
from the cupped palm of a modest
earth, smoothing her skirt.

. . .

But there, too, I have been unjust,
asking the bird to disavow
his jaunty beauty, rose mallow to flower
rue. Wanting to be fair—

let me trade it for plain
delight. Let me quit shaming

the flame-like things
or, at least, let the wind
unwinding its argon sarong
not mind the likes of me.

YMCA

The man who sells us pizza
moonlights here, lambasting
women on stationary bikes

up imaginary hills. His class,
my friend says, always fills.
There is something touching

about this: a man's unwanted
flair for browbeating
transformed into an asset at last.

I know some misery finds
the Y, too. A beginner folded
into a gi's starch cries.

Round kids and rangy kids
climb out of the pool in tees
that cling, a second skin

more conspicuous than skin.
Outside the tiny door
to a racquetball court, an EMT,

a wheeled cot. But it is easy,
scoured by these borrowed
towels, to love the others.

In chair yoga, the old
throw their arms slowly
open. A teenager teaches

a child to swim. The lifters
take turns standing over
each other, heaviness

between them. And the girl
whose parents made her come
with, who finds a treadmill

among the stalwart walkers
and the distance runners
ice has forced indoors,

who plugs her headphones
into the TV and leans
on the machine, ass against

guardrail, eating Cheetos,
never even shuffling her feet—
her I might love most of all.

Jumper

Mostly I applaud and jealousy
is a splinter in my hand. Not
that I would call it an affliction.

Not that, if pressed, I wouldn't
admit the words jealousy and
splinter both run wide. Nothing

stings, after all. During the ovation
for the actor who makes me wipe
my eyes, an eyelash-sized envy;

for the painter, a green bristle
from a horsehair brush. Maybe
this, too, can be explained: maybe

the whisker of our own talent
is what itches when we clap. Never,
after all, have my palms tingled

cheering the jumper. The girls
who make high dives lamellophones,
the shooting guard pedaling thin air

over the key—I laud them empty
handed and flat footed, the same
as any witness to unattainable grace.

A Finding

A friend of my friend has gone on a trip
and hung himself in the woods.
That he hid
that departure inside another journey
does not seem strange to me. The desperate

are often considerate. He wanted to die
in a town where whoever found him
would not have to bear this, too:
already knowing his name.
I find myself

hoping that, if they had to cut the frozen
rope, they cut it close to the noose,
that a stranger took his weight in their arms—
or, failing that, that they took the branch

from the tree.

I find myself studying,
with awful gratitude, the back of my hand.
Time has blended the raised satin
into the otherwise ordinary wear

fickling over my knuckles.
The first time
I wanted to disappear, I started small.
I took an eraser's pink oblique angles
to the base of my first finger. I wanted

to take a branch from a tree. I wanted
to hide inside another journey.
                                        The burn
of course made me more there. The scab
of course caught on the reinforced edge

of every pocket I tried to hide it in.
                                        I've given up,
now, on going out of turn, but I've found out:
the desperate are often considerate.

The Planetary Model of the Atom

The kids whose siblings lived minded it more;
they objected to matter loosely packed, to the molecule
more Calder mobile than puddingstone.

Or at least they marveled less how like a sun
a marble nucleus could ordain BBs for Bohr's orbits.

I'm not faulting them: what we want before grief
is to contain no absence; before grief we cannot guess
how much rides on the symmetry of heaven
and earth.

. . .

                    The kids whose siblings lived—
when they traced the textbook lacework of starches,
they felt only hunger; when they stared at the airy jumble
of a polymer like a fistful of unmatched jacks,
it was a reflex to test the desk's composite, to knock
and so surprise the world in its swiss density.

I am not mocking them, the uninitiated,
for being bewildered on learning these strange things:
how electrons that hula nuclei do not give,
how rapping on emptiness smarts.

Aphelion

In the stripe of grass between our sidewalk
and the astronomer's side of the street, a maple.

In October Larry emailed a picture of it, rich
as egg yolk; he was sorry we couldn't see the color

from his vantage point, a story up, studying
the stars in daylight. Often I think of asking him

things about light and gravity but choose instead
to hold onto my errant beliefs about the planets—

that they round the extremes of their orbits not
as swimmers tumble turning but as drinking birds,

the shift in their intentions no less delicate
and decisive than the toy tipplers' who, in top hats,

sip and abstain when two bulbs swap warmth.
But, really, what I don't want to give up is bigger:

the belief that everything that moves—worlds
and loves, swimmers and heat engines—is wise

to its aphelion; that we all have it in us
to feel an end coming and to turn right on time.

i Ways of Looking at a Blackbird

My son asks what entropy is
and the pepper
of matter shimmers wider

to warm the next emptiness,
universe-annexed.

                                        His brother
answers *If Order and Chaos*
from the Greek myths
were real

entropy would be
the science of those.

. . .

                                        Order goes
by Themis, really. She carries
and bears the Hours. She carries
a blade

            to hew fact
from fiction, to shave
the fat from fables—

a blade fit to split hairs—
sophists' grays—

a blade whet
to dissect fogs

but no sword
forged can bisect
an abyss.
What I mean is

there's an imaginary number
of ways to stare

at starlings,
the black birds
Chaos births,

and none is false
and none true.

. . .

My son asks
what entropy is and the sky fills

with murmuration,
with a Poincaré map.

His brother
bends over math worksheets

full of right answers wreathed
in unreal runes. *If* he says

and *If* throws the switches
on charm quarks, turning

some share of them strange.

Synchrony

Some, brought up to oratory, can pen
entreaties of any duration—pleas to last

a hundred last breaths, pleas five casualties
long. *In the time I've been speaking,*

the samaritan reads, and then it's the dead:
ninety of hunger, three swept out to sea.

Missionaries on the Sunday School junket
pass the plate. *Malaria has killed a dozen kids,*

they say, *in the time this slide show's taken.* I think
The lives a shorter speech could save.

I want never to say another word.

I know, I know. But it's hard to uncouple

the synchronous, the pitch and its perished, hard
to believe you will add nothing to death

by metering your speech against its rattle.
After a lecture on Milgram's experiment,

I dreaded the one lightswitch in the house
that seemed to turn nothing off or on:

how could my finger on the toggle dodge
the instant some stranger fell down dead?

I know. To name a simultaneity is not
to have a hand in it.

. . .

In the time I've been writing, the purslane
has set out the bees' yellow bowls.

Memento Vivere

My husband tells me I should write about life, about the garden
he's planted: the celosia topped with felted flames, the chenille
full of muppets' pink fingers. And it is not negligible, the life,

the marigolds crowding the touch-me-nots, the squash blossoms
like nylon try-on socks stashed in a plant we didn't mean to buy.
If it must be life, let me also mention the cardinal. He's gargling

song at the top of a dogwood my husband stands under
with an orb of waning geranium in his hand, and I,
who have told many half-truths, say, *But I always write about life.*

Still Life With

There is nothing with which
you can still life.
Even so, the painter strives
in his atelier to ransom hams
from perishability

and greater his art
who can garnish the dish
gone off
with a blood-sozzled fly.

Less stunning are the lobsters
and fish in sequin sheaths
and mundane
is the unplucked duck
that dangles on the wall.

. . .

There is nothing with which
you can still life.
Even the veriest vase
in trompe-l'oeil
is subject to cracks
under lacquer

as sure as silver ewers cloud
and handmade goblets drip

because sand-made
glass is viscous,

a deserter
who waits and waits.

. . .

There is nothing with which
you can still life.
Even the twin halves
of fruits ferment
and peaches' cheeks
go weak
as the jowls of a gran
who takes her dentures out.

Art cannot halt
this lavish thing
that pockmarks
lemon peels.

With life still so unsated
and so corruptible,
nothing, nothing
can still it,
shifty iridescent life.

Different Stillness

Dead, an animal has a different stillness, an indifferent
stillness; the rigor of creatures in copses, sniffing the air,
is a surer stiffness than that of their stiffs, their corpses
in rigor mortis. In life, hognose and hose, pill bug and pill:

they are interchangeable. In death, an animal is softer,
lumpier, less still. Across the water, I cannot tell what
is bobbing in the river, but I can tell it is neither buoy
nor log. I mean, I cannot tell who is bobbing in the water,

but soon the current bears me to where I can make out
the deer's ear, and I think, Once the fawn would have
pointed that ballet slipper and heard us, the danger we all
are—what with our vehicles, what with our metaphors.

Oddest and Oldest and Saddest and Best

My student spends his summers in city cemeteries,
clipping the scruff that grows too close to the stones

or anywhere the mowers can't go. Sundays mostly

the death-jilted come, some to pledge the stiff
with a fifth, some to Windex the pane of granite.
Some of those left
come to sob nearer the leaver
or, anyway, nearer
the dregs that pool in their defector's chest.

Sundays my student stays home.
Mondays he finds the flat and shouldered bottles.
He finds a silver pita barely levitating
in the cool of the day,
bleeding helium molecules. The remnant
trapped in the Mylar
huddles small for warmth. He finds

that those who visit the hours he works
don't mind the loose orbit
the groundskeepers keep
around their mellowed grief.

He tells me about the priest
who lingers after giving a graveside homily
heavy on Jonah. *The Lord appoints*
the bush and the worm that attacks
the bush.

Some of the bereaved, my student says,
regain their curiosity. They ask him
about the others' epitaphs: oddest and oldest
and saddest and best.

Fourfold Amen

Onstage, it takes the lead
a lot of words to die. Maybe
I, too, am holding a red scarf
to a false wound.

. . .

This morning someone
published a how-to titled
Telling Your Kids
It's the End of the World.

Maybe there's been a run
on red scarves that pool,
silken, sanguine,
in actors' laps. Either that
or button tips no longer
come with épées.

. . .

I am not ungrateful
for the last lecture, for letters
labeled *in the event of*,
for the lawyers
who write up our wills;
every lullay I've sung—
I've meant it.

. . .

But I would rather go out
stringing a hymn along,
singing to delay the end
of men, rolling the first letter
up the octaves again
and again.

I would rather be the sort
who cannot help
but run back and duck
her head inside
a rolled-down window
for another kiss
before life pulls away.

III

Go Back to Your Own Country

Let me tell you about countries: nobody has their own
and where we come from moves. Our mothers' wombs
aren't where we left them. Continents calve. Jerusalem holds
a tray full of glasses that a scrum of men take
and put back, take and put back, unworried for the weight
she must shift. Let me tell you: some of our countries
aren't where we left them. Someone pulls a string and six
tumble from Yugoslavia's pocket. Someone halves
Sudan like a branch over their knee. Someone crumbles
a bailey between Berlins and Germany is one place
again. Only Adam had his own country, and he could not
go back. A country is land that's learned to disown.

I drive to prison

where the tallest man in class speaks of children
who trip and stand up unhurt and do not cry

until they see broken skin, carnelian, a trickle
shaped like a run in a stocking. He says

we're like that still, that there is a sickness a man
can catch just catching his likeness in a glass.

. . .

Down my street lives a salesman whose wife died.
Once a week he putters past on his Vespa, a grandson

braced between his knees. For months the kid
would not loose the handlebars to wave.

. . .

Sometimes beauty lets you forget yourself. I drive
to prison early. At that hour, day can hardly see

over earth's shoulder. At that hour, vapor: stoneflies
airbrushing the river's patchy complexion,

brown shapes grazing. But I meant to tell you about a place
where the road curves, and I, following, steer

toward brilliance. I know the wish is foolish. I wish
I could drive my student to this bend in the route

I take east, to the spot where a rampart of forest
absorbs the sun's first blows, where the trees cannot

swallow the shining in time. He would stretch one
long arm out the window, I think. And no longer shy

of the car's side mirrors, he would, no less than the oaks
conquered by light, forget himself and be anointed.

Shambles & Sons

One way to sum us up—all of us, I mean—
is to survey the mess we've made.
I'm not saying there's nothing lovely left.

I'm saying that in Europe there are fields
where buttercups know not to breach
the rims of bomb craters and in Antarctica

there are birds who don't know bottlecaps
from clams. And while it's impossible
to know how it started—Shambles & Sons—

whether as an observatory or armory, Adam
died a factotum: zookeeper, embalmer,
architect, priest. Well, from there we took

on a life of our own. We took lives. We gave
birth. And suddenly there were
middens and archives, caesars and towers,

electricity, antiquities, theaters, mines.
Before we knew it, Earthshine
was a movie we'd projected on the moon.

We said humankind was too big to fail.
Rash Shambles, we said the sun
would never set on the Anthropocene.

For Dean, on His Shift

Between standing guard and bearing witness,
your sleeplessness. Part of the work is waiting—

for the furnace, winded, to rest; for the garage
to yawn around the sedan borrowed by a child—

and part of the work is readiness, as if low-grade
grief could bamboozle tragedy, as if the one fate

that could not take your dear ones was the one
you let loom, a premonition in the dark. Mostly,

though, you know that you are keeping watch
only in the loosest sense. You did not interrupt

the drifter who rifled your truck and found it
wanting, the kids who overshot the crab apples

with rolls of toilet paper, who decked every
runged or limbed thing with white crepe

that rainbowed and collapsed. And you do not
chase the deer from the garden. You let them be.

You tell me that night is your shift, that it has
always been your shift, no other way to explain it,

and I want to say, I feel it too, all the loneliness
of childhood, all the loneliness of how late it is.

For Danny, Reading Poems

When I was a kid, only a flu could buy me
a screen cubed and populated. In morning,

the mugging Bradys, appraising one another
above and below, glancing summary judgments

through the lattice bordering their blue cells,
like a yearbook page come to dubious life.

In afternoon, an ennead of actors and comics
in Rubixed cubicles, a tic-tac-toe board:

nine rooms, mostly desk. And this is what
we thought of when the world got sick,

we who, now middle-aged, watched Jan slide
her siblings the side eye and Whoopi

wise-crack from a grid's center square.
It's what we made jokes about, seeing ourselves

populate cubed screens. That spring
we subscribed to Zoom and pretended

that we, too, were one thing: a family, a troupe.
In illness, you do what you must. You build

the dollhouse or dormitory a diorama at a time.
Tonight I am listening to my friend read poems.

Here it is the hour before dark. There, too—
a high window turns cobalt behind him—

but not everywhere. On the first floor, a man
in an apron makes a late supper, his back

to an obsidian pane, and on the third is
a yellow room, a woman capped in sunlight.

When I was a kid, I wished the Bradys
would lean past the sashes of their squares

and chat across the matrix of that rookery;
I wished the Hollywood types would visit,

would exit their kit-cat portraits and cross
the shotgun tenement, the game show's set.

And for us, too, I want this trespass: egress.
I want the courtyard our quarters overlook.

I want the illicit bonfire lit in the cube of air
that belongs to all of us, or none.

For Richard—with Love and Squalor

Lodestone for gutter wonders—for Incredibles
flown through rolled-down windows; for rubberband

strands of stranded pearls; for road-rash baseballs;
for birthday candles, wicks still white. Sommelier

of nectars, bee balm telegram-man, summer courier
of jelly-bean sedum.
                                        You deliver a garden's pate

in a cake pan, and I work my fingers under the dirt
backing the beaded turf. You tell me it will take

wherever I set it down.
                                        If I wrote stories, I would begin
with you, rigging magic lanterns from colanders,

hanging mirror-work pennants from pergolas,
teaching vines to candy-stripe. I would begin with you,

chakra-stamped, cycling away with a nursery's worth:
a tiny tin-can maple in your backpack's starboard pocket;

blanket flower port; and strapped to you like an infant,
ditch lilies, an armful, another wildness not to waste.

Harvest in the Dark

In therapy, I lay my cards on the table:
ace of briefcases and reverse hermit, jack
of all trades, queen of wind-up dolls.
I play a tornado, a Garbage Pail Kid,
the five of cups. I am still trying to change.

When I started this work, I thought the well
willed themselves stable, pulling whatever
their edges were toward a middle or a mean,
that they'd learned to solve for averages.

I wanted what was average, too. I figured
I could split the difference, that halfway
between the self who did not want to wake
or wash and the one who over-functioned
there must be a middle-aged woman
in jeans, getting on with what was.

But a mother who rages because it's all
too much—famine and swimming lessons,
bees dying, her boys checking
each others' necks for ticks—and the child
who cries because nothing is enough—
neither art nor protests—cannot come
to any entente, death being proof for both.

Because the mother is right and the child is right.
A hermit cannot take a queen or a tornado
an ace. I am still trying to change. Listen,

between what is diametrical there is a field
of rhubarb growing so fervently that it creaks,
and to preserve its sweetness, farmers harvest it
in nothing harsher than moon- or candlelight.

Washing the Corpses

These two dead painted themselves
before a mirror, but now, flour-dusted, they blush

under the powder, less than bloodless,
and because it's my eyeshadow that shadows

their cheeks, gaunt for a night, those hollows
also shimmer, belied by porch lights—

so mostly my sons hold pillowcases open
before neighbors who are bemused by their piebald,

expectant faces. More convincing is the kohl
that these bright-eyed corpses

have daubed at their blinking, rehearsing
the dark sockets that they will age into

and sleeplessness deepen, until its ash
sets, a pall more permanent than embalmers' glue.

. . .

Of course I pray that these two dead
will live forever. I pray it as I swab kohl

from their blinking, absorbing the false decease,
and I pray it as under lavender lantern-jaws

I find my children's familiar chins. Caked
on the washcloth, a cadaverous paste, and I cannot

scrub them pink enough, but I do spare
their lips, licorice-red, and kiss them goodnight

and pray: God, spare these corpses of an hour.
I have washed them back just into mortality.

Care

After my second son was born, I bled
and bled. I apologized to the nurses
for the mess I was making, and they
shushed me, and that was also love.

Yesterday two women recited
their fears for their teenage children
while punching samples of tissue
from the darkness hidden at the back

of a small jello, my left breast.
And if it was surreal for me, lying
there, a pane of orchard and sky
in the ceiling overhead, still: theirs

was the kindness that plies silence,
where mortal fear could multiply,
with the mundane: driver's training,
summer jobs. Now I'm waiting.

Whatever happens—when I stood
a nurse tied my gown for me
and reached behind me to slide
the medal on my necklace

to the front, that and the tiny charms
stamped with the first letters of my sons'
names—whatever happens, I've been held
by gentle and competent hands.

Shroud

In the old poem, a woman unravels
at night what she weaves by day—

a beautiful conceit, even if mostly
things just undo themselves. A day

before the biopsy, my therapist asks
me to tell a story about the next day.

So I close my eyes and imagine rising,
rousing my sons—*Is it nexterday?*

one used to ask, meaning tomorrow.
I say: here is the list of Wednesday

extras (trumpet, singlet). I say: I will
badger their shoes on, singing *To-da-ay*,

and if next I wave down the car and kiss
my boys' palms, they won't think *Today*

we might come home to bad news—
because I am always like this; every day,

the same harried love. But also:
in this poem, a woman unravels at night.

A Theodicy for Children

God is the precipice
and theodicy the gravity
for the cataract of *why*s
Matroyshka-ed inside
a child. Why does
the car stop, why
is the light red, why
do people register
that color as warning

and there it is: blood
in the water, again,
again.
          A child
does not ask why not
bundle our arteries
farther from our surfaces,
does not blame God
for what seem to be
our flesh's design flaws—
even as they teethe.

That is our part.
I have wanted to damn
the God I could not move.
I have wanted to dam
my sons' rivers of whys.

A theodicy for children:
why is a waterfall
and all that entails.

My Sadness Is Complete

To say some things, it both is and is not
too late. For a month, I wait on an opening
in the radiologist's schedule. All that time
my worry, a girl with huge front teeth, reads
over my shoulder. I do not push her away.

And after the biopsy comes back clean,
she goes of her own accord, returning to a room
with plaid walls. In that room, our brothers
are beaming: one white-blond and knee-high;
one thin, limbs akimbo, and wearing a red cap,

which means he is already dying. Of course
it is and is not too late to follow her, to say
that they are not pretending, that they are happy,
to say that sometimes we were—even if
for forty years I have remembered the first night

of Adam's sickness better than any other thing:
the strange sauce on my grandma's pasta,
the strange sheets on my dad's boyhood bed,
and Luke on my left, small and asleep. I watched
him so hard. Well, there was never any telling

the kids in that room a single thing: not that
if vigilance could have saved their brother,
he would not be dead; not that if worry
could have saved him, he would be immortal.
So it follows that for weeks, I worried myself.

But at last my sadness is complete. Older than
the parents who lost you, old enough to estimate
how unfair and how brave, I say, forgive me
for swimming, for looking away. It is not too late.
I say, forgive me for wanting to love you less.

Stay tender somehow,

Dina writes, and I pick up my pencil. I wish
I could call the place it comes to rest, the small
and grooved knob on my fourth finger, a cradle

but it is a callus, stubborn as an uncooked lentil.
I think about my grandmother's sleeping gloves,
about how my aunt could not be entirely gentle

jimmying her mother's embalmed fingers
into their silk, appointed tunnels, saying
She never slept soundly without them.

I think about the tiny mitts that keep infants
from scratching their faces, about how my sons
napping in summer looked like prize-fighters

felled—high-waisted diapers and flimsy shorts,
hands balled inside gauntlets. Some blessings
fire and backfire so sweetly. *Stay tender* is one.

NOTES

Three of the poems in this collection borrow from other writers' titles: "On Beauty and Being Just" from Elaine Scarry (verbatim) and, slightly less directly, "*i* Ways of Looking at a Blackbird" and "For Richard—with Love and Squalor" from Wallace Stevens and J.D. Salinger, respectively.

ACKNOWLEDGMENTS

Many of the poems in this book owe happy debts to the people in them. So: thank you, Sarah, Bruce, Mel, Kevin, Karl, and Hannah. Thank you, Carlon. And thank you, Dean Ward, Danny Lawless, Richard Smith, Krista List Leinberger, Larry Molnar, and Dina L. Relles.

Thank you to Calvin University for the provision of a sabbatical, for the chance to spend time with the students who are among my most reliable sources of hope, and for putting me in the proximity of smart and kind colleagues. A particular word of gratitude to Kristine Johnson (I know that sending people poems is no way to make or keep friends, but you are the lucky, brilliant exception) and Jennifer L. Holberg, who has been waiting for me to land a book contract with the most loyal sort of impatience.

My thanks to my closest poetry kin. Christian Wiman, your words have been indispensable to me, and I'll never be able to thank you enough for that or for the wild gift of your reading my poems and finding a book in there. Amit Majmudar, you gave so many of the poems in this book their titles, and you dared me to be more prolific and then taught me how—thank you. W.J. Herbert, thank you for the master class in sequencing manuscripts and for the many encouragements you've sent my way. Peter Vertacnik and Maya C. Popa, thank you for blessing my words on their way. And Luke Hankins, thank you for taking a chance on my manuscript, as well as for lending me your eye and ear and all the resources of Orison Books.

Thank you to my family. John and Nancy Knol: a poet could not ask to be born to better parents, to people more generous with story and beauty and language. Abel and Carrie Zwart: a poet could not ask to marry into better parents; I know you're proud of me, and I'm proud of you, too. Thank you to my brother Luke, who—along with his wife Corina and son Elliott—has kept me such funny and tender company. Thank you to my brother Adam: missing you has taught me so much of what I know about the heart. And thank you to my sons, Wendell and Amby, whose wisdom and astonishment I often borrow. Most of all, thank you to my husband, Andrew, who could tell me to be less sensitive but instead helps me to be brave.

You too, reader. Thank you.

Finally, thank you to the very early readers of many of this collection's poems for giving them a first home.

32 Poems: "On Beauty and Being Just"
Alaska Quarterly Review: "*i* Ways of Looking at a Blackbird"
Amsterdam Review: "Shambles & Sons"
Anti-heroin Chic: "Shroud"
Aquifer (Florida Review Online): "Used Benison"
Bad Lilies: "Morbid Children"
basalt: "Still Life With"
Bear Review: "Harvest in the Dark"
The Bellingham Review: "Washing the Corpses"
Berlin Lit: "Midlife Crisis"
Columba: "My childhood was not an agony"
Contemporary Verse 2: "Go Back to Your Own Country"
The Cortland Review: "Stay Tender Somehow"
HAD: "Long Distance"
Juxtaprose: "For Richard—with Love and Squalor"
Maine Review: "YMCA"
The Moth: "Bad news finds you where it finds you,"
One Hand Clapping: "I drive to prison"

On the Seawall: "Fourfold Amen"
Ploughshares: "Oddest and Oldest and Saddest and Best"
Plume: "For Danny, Reading Poems," "Learning to Read"
Poetry: "All my life I was a bride married to amazement"
Poetry Northwest: "Life Imitates"
The Poetry Review: "A Finding"
Radar: "For Dean, on His Shift," "The Planetary Model of the Atom"
Saranac Review: "Aphelion," "Different Stillness," "A Theodicy for Children"
Shenandoah: "Jumper"
South Carolina Review: "Poem with a Hole In It"
Southeast Review: "Pink Noise Machine"
The Southern Review: "Waiting Room"
Superstition Review: "Synchrony"
wildness: "I read that the moon is rusting"
Worcester Review: "Memento Vivere"

ABOUT THE AUTHOR

Jane Zwart teaches literature and writing at Calvin University, where she also co-directs the Calvin Center for Faith & Writing. Her poems have appeared widely in periodicals, including *Poetry*, *The Poetry Review*, *Ploughshares*, *The Southern Review*, and *Threepenny Review*.

ABOUT ORISON BOOKS

Orison Books is a 501(c)3 non-profit literary press focused on the life of the spirit from a broad and inclusive range of perspectives. We seek to publish books of exceptional poetry, fiction, and non-fiction from perspectives spanning the spectrum of spiritual and religious thought, ethnicity, gender identity, and sexual orientation.

As a non-profit literary press, Orison Books depends on the support of donors. To find out more about our mission and our books, or to make a donation, please visit www.orisonbooks.com.

Orison Books is deeply grateful to our recurring annual donors for sustaining our important work. If you'd like to make a recurring or one-time contribution, please visit www.orisonbooks.com/support-us.

Sustainers' Circle

Carol Dines
Keith Flynn
Michele Laub
Laura & Barry Rand
Bruce Spang
Lee Stockdale

Advocates' Circle

David Ebenbach
Anonymous

Supporters' Circle

Nickole Brown
Richard Chess

Friends' Circle

Paige Gilchrist
Laurel Haavik
Alida Woods